Important

If you find a wildlife animal in need, please contact a wildlife rescue group or obtain a wildlife license, as trained wildlife rehabilitators are equipped to provide the necessary care and assistance.

Evi is a mini-Schnauzer who guards the backyard. She pretends to be brave, but the slightest noise sends her into hiding. The only sound she loves is the snap, crackle, pop of cereal pouring into a bowl.

Ally, my Golden Retriever, is sweet and always happy. She runs with a playful hop in her step. She is pretty laid back, unless you have a ham and cheese sandwich.

Cade, Will and Rhyan,

I am incredibly proud of all of you. Always believe in yourself and chase your dreams. Know your worth and make the world a better place!

Love you forever,

Mom

Christi Harvey Books

CREATED WITH HUMAN INTELLIGENCE

MY 3 SQUIRRELS

The Rescue
(with a Twist)

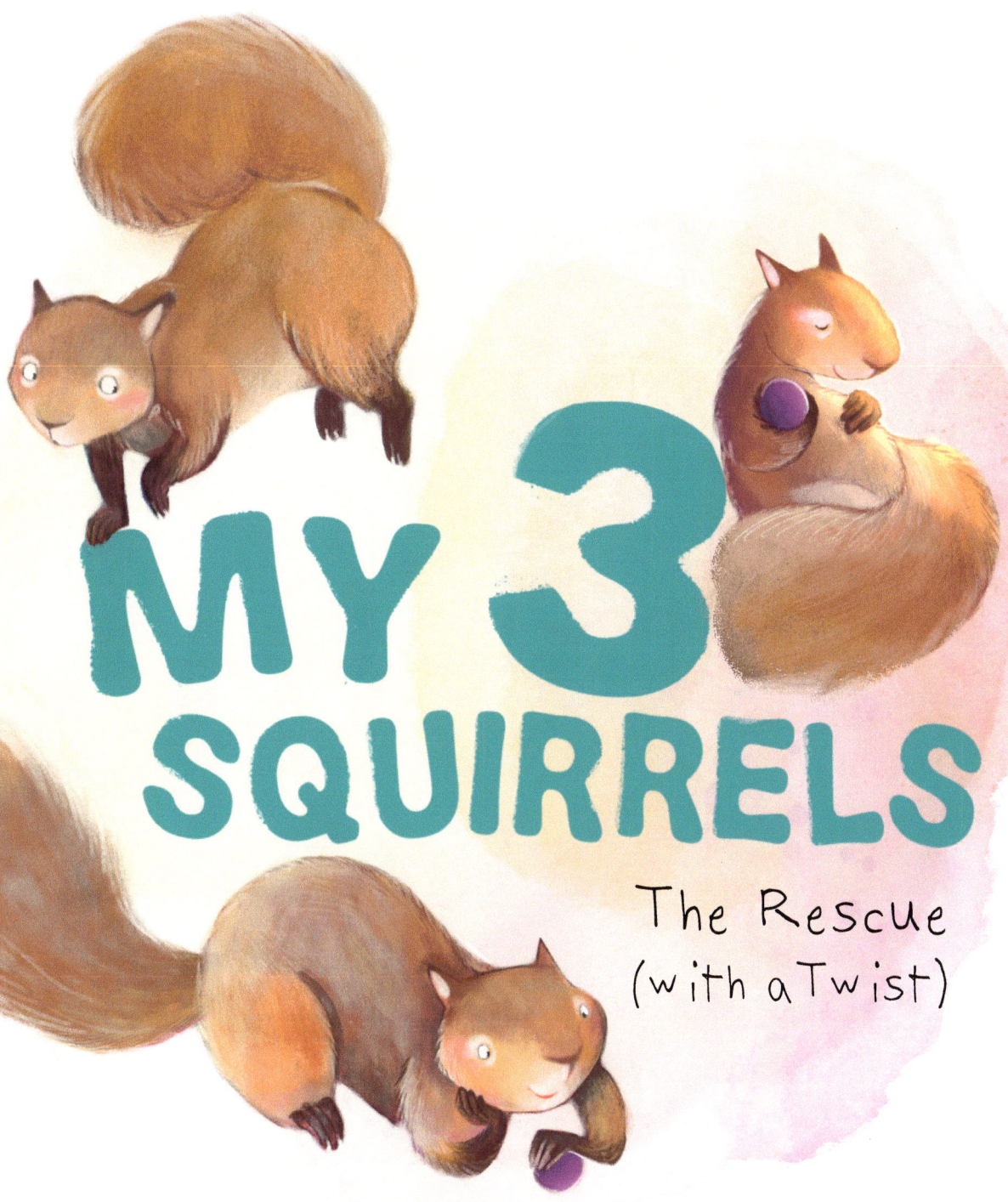

Written by Christi Harvey - Illustrated by Stella Maris

As I sat on my back patio one August day, a light drizzle floated to the ground. Humidity is the sworn enemy of curly hair.

In one chaotic

POOF

I was a dandelion in full bloom.

Heavy rain
    started
and the wind
    was blowing onto
    Ally's face.

Branches snapped
and leaves whirled
in a messy dance!

"It's a

twister

I yelled.

"Let's get inside,
girls!"

We huddled in a corner
until the wind and rain
stopped.

I opened the door and…

It looked like Mother Nature had a temper tantrum!

The neighbor's roof was torn off, wooden fences
ripped up and scattered,
and the wooden bench
in a pile.
Even the top of our
oak tree was gone!

"We need a beaver clean-up
crew to help with this mess."

Suddenly, a tiny, furry face peeked out
from the pine needles—then two more!

"It's three baby squirrels!" I said.

Their parents were nowhere around.
I gently picked up the nest with a towel.

"What should I do? Their eyes aren't
even open." I wondered.

I imagined feeding them and becoming a
family. I knew I had to care for them.

Evi and Ally followed me inside,
where the squirrels were safe.

One
morning,

after weeks of caring
for the squirrels,

I walked into
the room...

...to see three
furry faces
looking at me.

I was the first person they saw!

"I will call them ...

Crosby,

"Crosby, you must
help your little
brother and sister
find food and water
once you are released
back to nature."

Scooter

and Nutmeg!"

"Scooter, you are small but mighty. You zoom around like a scooter! You will teach your brother and sister to jump through the trees with speed and precision."

"Nutmeg, you are sweet and playful. Teach others how to play fair, trust your instincts and be kind along the way!"

Raising three squirrels is like...

...feeding three hungry teenagers.

Get the blueberry pizzas ready and *cut the cheese*! Squirrels have a *strict* diet.

Months later, after caring for and feeding the squirrels, their fur got thicker and their tails got fluffier. It was time for them to return to the world they were meant for.

So, I started collecting wood and branches ...

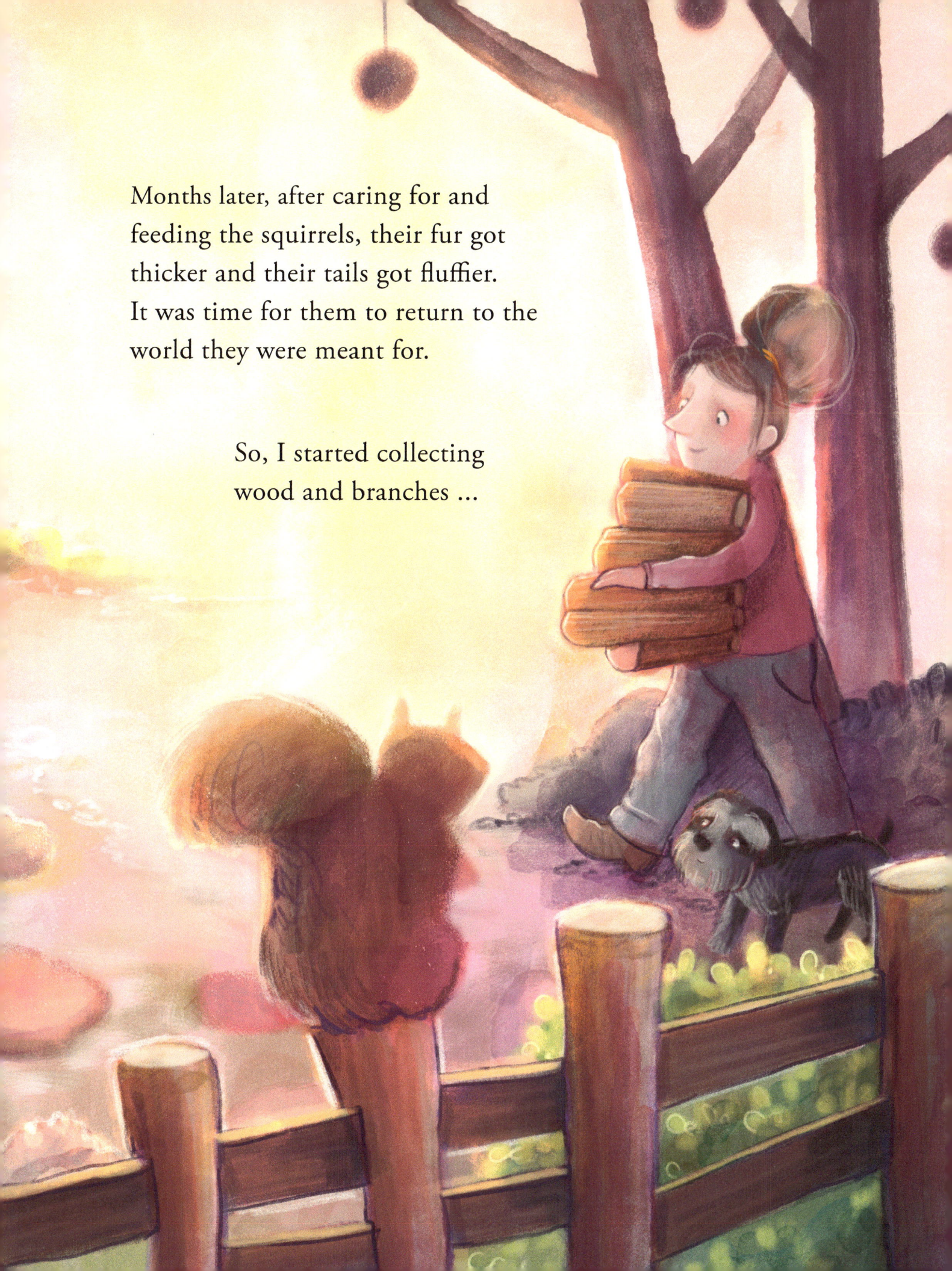

... to build

bang!

an outdoor
house

bang!

for Crosby, Scooter
and Nutmeg.

CROSBY
SCOOTER

My smile stretched
across my face as I moved
the squirrels to their
new home.

bang!

I left the
door open
so they could
come and go
freely!

SQUIRREL
LAND

Oh, how they love
being outside!

They know where to
go for the yummy
food and can visit me
every day.

They even look
through the back door
to see where I am.

The outdoors brought new
adventures. They have new
friends! They play in the trees,
run the fence line, climb the
bird feeders, and hide nuts
all over the backyard.

I can whistle from anywhere and they will come.
Their tiny paws and bushy tails,
flicking with curiosity, fill my heart.

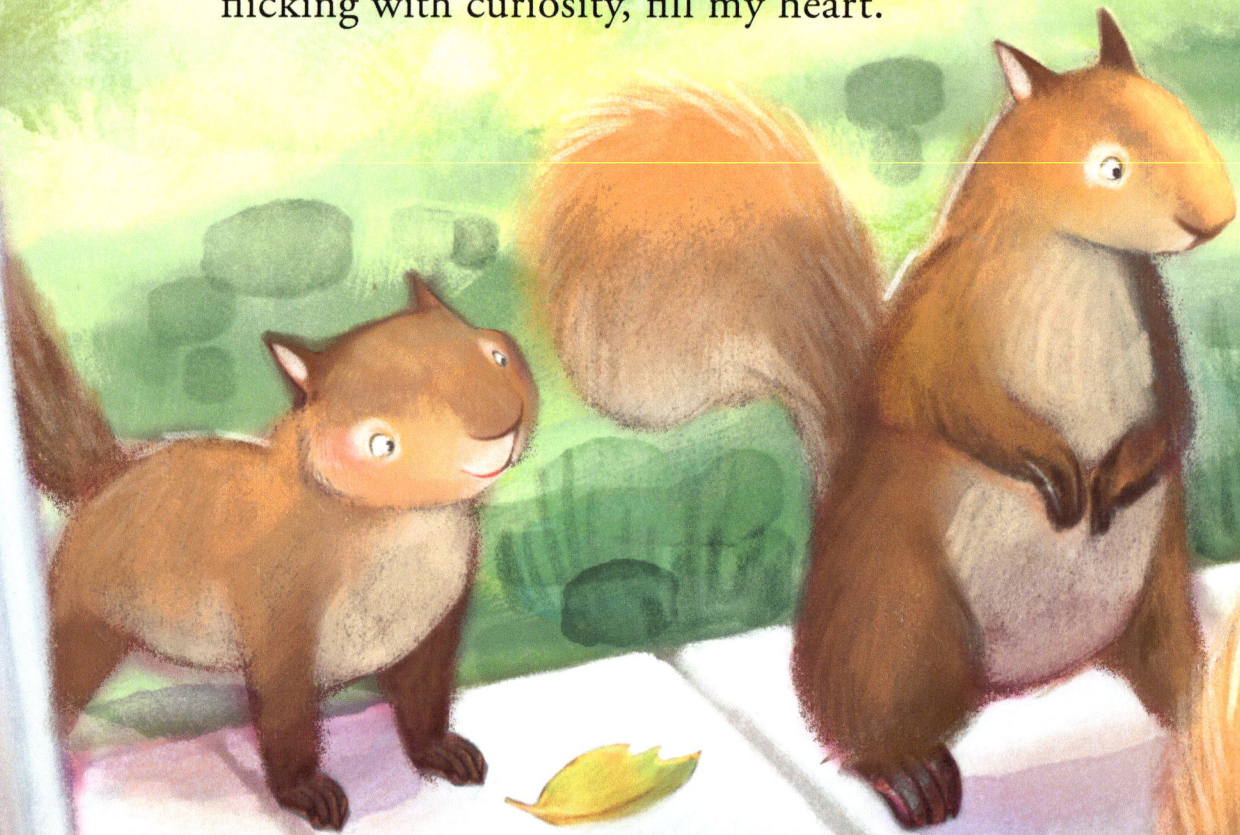

They are free but
still part of my family.

They know me and trust me.
I loved raising
my three squirrels.

It's like three tiny, furry whirlwinds
stopping by for a cuddle.

You better have snacks
in your pocket to share!

I don't have a tail or fur, but our hearts match!
I gave Crosby, Scooter and Nutmeg the gift of life.

They gave me the joy of watching
them live it freely!

Crosby and Scooter have buried a nut, but they can't remember exactly how to find it!

Can you help them solve the maze without waking up Mr. Mole?

Christi Harvey

is a children's book author and lifelong animal lover from Lake Charles, Louisiana. Inspired by the real-life rescue of three baby squirrels, her latest book "My 3 Squirrels" celebrates the magic of animal rescue, nature, and the unexpected bonds that change our lives. With guidance from a veterinarian, Christi helped raise and release the orphaned squirrels, who now visit with playful energy and joy.

Wife and mother of three, Christi draws from her own adoption story to explore themes of belonging, connection, and bonds—both in her writing and in her life. Though she lost her beloved dog Ally during the writing of this book, Ally's loyal spirit lives on.

My 3 Squirrels is Christi's second children's book.
Follow them on social media or
visit www.christiharveybooks.com

Squirrel
APPROVED

www.ingramcontent.com/pod-product-compliance
Lightning Source LLC
Chambersburg PA
CBHW041545260326
41914CB00015B/1554